In the Country

Ben Butterworth

On the Farm

Then

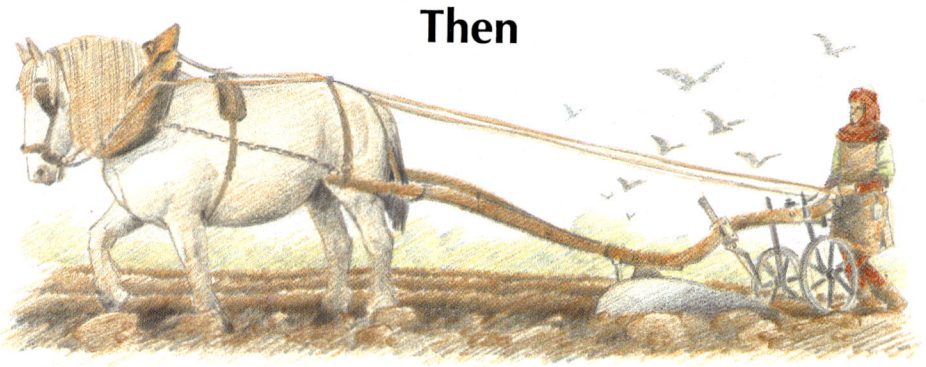

A plough used to be pulled by a horse or an ox. It only made one furrow at a time.

Corn used to be cut by hand. The farm worker used a scythe or sickle to do this.

A flail was used to hit the corn so that all the seed dropped out. This is called threshing.

Cows were often milked in the fields. The farmer used a wooden yoke so that he could carry two heavy buckets full of milk.

Now

A modern plough can make 8 furrows at a time. This makes ploughing much quicker.

A combine harvester does many things. It cuts the corn and threshes it. The seed and the straw are separated.

Electric machines can now milk lots of cows.

Birds in Town and Country

Cuckoo

You can hear cuckoos call in April. A cuckoo does not make a nest but lays eggs in the nest of another bird.

Tawny owl

Tawny owls fly at night, so not many people have seen one.

Starling

Sometimes in the evening you can see and hear hundreds of starlings resting in one tree. The mess they make can kill the tree.

Robin

Robins seem to be friendly birds. They come close when you dig the garden. Robins can be nasty to other birds.

House Martin

House martins fly in from Africa in the spring. They can fly at over 40 miles an hour.

Kestrel

Kestrels feed on mice and other small animals. They hover in the air and then swoop down. Kestrels can swoop down at 125 miles an hour.

Wild Animals

Hedgehog

Baby hedgehogs have soft spines. After three weeks the spines become prickly. The hedgehog sleeps in the day and hunts for food at night.

Bat

Bats go to sleep hanging upside down. Bats fly like birds but they do not build nests or lay eggs.

Fox

Foxes live in a hole in the ground. This is called an earth. A fox will kill lots of chickens then only eat one of them.

Squirrel

Squirrels can be seen in towns as well as in the country. A squirrel's home is called a drey.

Rabbit

Rabbits live under the ground. They make lots of tunnels. Lots of rabbits live together.

Mouse

Mice can live almost anywhere. A female mouse can have as many as 100 babies each year.

Wild Flowers

Bluebell

Bluebells grow in woods as well as in fields. Sometimes bluebells are white.

Dandelion

Dandelions grow everywhere. Do you know what a dandelion clock is? If you find one what do you do with it?

Honeysuckle

Honeysuckle grows in hedges. It smells sweet. At night you can often see moths in honeysuckle.

Primrose

Primroses grow in woods and on banks. Next time you go on a train in the spring, look out for primroses growing by the side of the railway track.

Rosebay Willow Herb

Rosebay willow herb will grow almost anywhere. You often find this plant where there has been a fire. The flowers at the bottom of the stem open first.

Poppy

Poppies grow in fields and by the road-side. You will often see bees visiting the bright red flowers.

Trees

Trees are the largest plants in the world. Trees that lose all their leaves in the autumn are called deciduous. Trees that keep their leaves all the year are called evergreen.

Oak

Oak trees can grow to a very large size and live a very long time. Lots of insects live in an oak tree. The seed of an oak tree is called an acorn.

Sycamore

There are lots of sycamore trees growing in the countryside. Each leaf has five points like a hand. The seeds spin down and look rather like a helicopter flying.

Plane

You often see plane trees along the side of busy streets. Plane trees are planted in towns because they don't mind all the dust.

Pine

The pine tree has thin leaves which stay on the tree in the winter. The fruit of a pine tree is called a cone. This opens in dry weather and closes when it is wet.

Horse chestnut

The horse chestnut tree has large pink or white flowers in the spring. The bees love them. Why do children love horse chestnut trees?

When a tree dies, it leaves a stump in the ground which goes rotten. Some insects and plants love rotten tree stumps. How many can you see in the picture?

Butterflies

A butterfly passes through four stages in its life.

The eggs are laid on a leaf.

An egg turns into a caterpillar.

The caterpillar turns into a chrysalis.

The chrysalis turns into a butterfly.

Orange Tip

Look for orange tips in May and June. Butterflies use their colours to find each other.

Large White

Look for large whites between May and August. The caterpillars eat cabbage plants and do a lot of damage.

Red Admiral

Red admirals are large butterflies. They can be seen all through the summer. Like all butterflies they only live a few weeks.

Peacock

Sometimes in the winter you can find a peacock butterfly hiding in an old shed. In the summer you can see them on stinging nettles.

The Country Code

1. Look after all wildlife, wild plants and trees.
2. Close all gates when you walk in the country.
3. Keep dogs on a lead. They can worry sheep and chickens.
4. Keep to paths across farmland.

5   Leave no litter behind.
6   Keep all water clean.
7   Do not damage fences, hedges and walls.
8   Go carefully on country roads.
9   Leave crops, machinery and livestock alone.

If you look at this picture carefully, you will see that some people are breaking the country code. Can you find all the things that they shouldn't be doing?

Nature Records

Keep a record of all the wild flowers, birds, animals and trees you see.

List the flowers by colours. Then you can find out which colour has the most flowers.

Draw the leaves of the trees and put the names of the trees beside them.

Make a note of when and where you see any wild animals and birds.

Don't forget the butterflies.

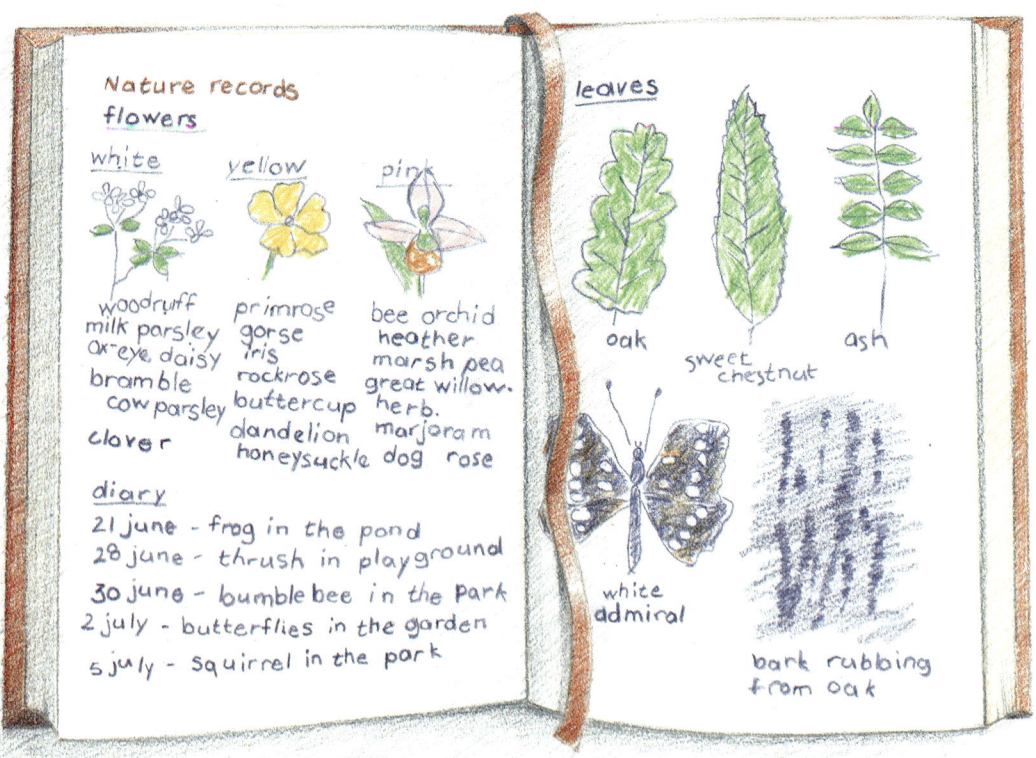